GARDENING LOGBOOK

This Book Bloges To

GARDENING LOGBOOK

NAME	LOCATION
SUPPLIER	PRICE

SCIENTIFIC CLASS

VEGETABLE	○	FRUIT
HERB	○	FLOWER
SHRUB	○	TREE
ANNUAL	○	BIENNIAL
PERENNIAL	○	SEEDLING

DATES

GERMINATED

PLANTED

HARVESTED

LIGHT LEVEL

SUN

PARTIAL SUN

SHADE

OTHER

STARTED FROM

SEED

PLANT

RATING

SIZE	○○○○○
COLOR	○○○○○
TASTE	○○○○○

FERTILIZERS & EQUIPMENT

_____

_____

_____

_____

_____

WATER REQUIREMENTS

0%
LESS

CARE INSTRUCTIONS

_____

_____

_____

_____

PLANTING INSTRUCTION

_____

_____

_____

_____

ADDITIONAL NOTES

_____

_____

_____

_____

_____

_____

_____

GARDENING LOGBOOK

NAME	LOCATION
SUPPLIER	PRICE

SCIENTIFIC CLASS

- VEGETABLE ○
- HERB ○
- SHRUB ○
- ANNUAL ○
- PERENNIAL ○

- FRUIT
- FLOWER
- TREE
- BIENNIAL
- SEEDLING

DATES

GERMINATED

PLANTED

HARVESTED

LIGHT LEVEL

SUN

PARTIAL SUN

SHADE

OTHER

STARTED FROM

SEED

PLANT

RATING

SIZE ○○○○○

COLOR ○○○○○

TASTE ○○○○○

FERTILIZERS & EQUIPMENT

_____

_____

_____

_____

_____

WATER REQUIREMENTS

0%
LESS

CARE INSTRUCTIONS

_____

_____

_____

_____

_____

PLANTING INSTRUCTION

_____

_____

_____

_____

ADDITIONAL NOTES

_____

_____

_____

_____

_____

_____

GARDENING LOGBOOK

NAME	LOCATION
SUPPLIER	PRICE

SCIENTIFIC CLASS

VEGETABLE	○	FRUIT
HERB	○	FLOWER
SHRUB	○	TREE
ANNUAL	○	BIENNIAL
PERENNIAL	○	SEEDLING

DATES

GERMINATED

PLANTED

HARVESTED

LIGHT LEVEL

SUN

PARTIAL SUN

SHADE

OTHER

STARTED FROM

SEED

PLANT

RATING

SIZE	○○○○○
COLOR	○○○○○
TASTE	○○○○○

FERTILIZERS & EQUIPMENT

_____

_____

_____

_____

_____

WATER REQUIREMENTS

0%
LESS

CARE INSTRUCTIONS

_____

_____

_____

_____

_____

PLANTING INSTRUCTION

_____

_____

_____

_____

ADDITIONAL NOTES

_____

_____

_____

_____

_____

_____

_____

GARDENING LOGBOOK

NAME	LOCATION
SUPPLIER	PRICE

SCIENTIFIC CLASS

- VEGETABLE ○
- HERB ○
- SHRUB ○
- ANNUAL ○
- PERENNIAL ○

- FRUIT
- FLOWER
- TREE
- BIENNIAL
- SEEDLING

DATES

GERMINATED

PLANTED

HARVESTED

LIGHT LEVEL

SUN

PARTIAL SUN

SHADE

OTHER

STARTED FROM

SEED

PLANT

RATING

SIZE ○○○○○

COLOR ○○○○○

TASTE ○○○○○

FERTILIZERS & EQUIPMENT

_____

_____

_____

_____

_____

WATER REQUIREMENTS

0%
LESS

CARE INSTRUCTIONS

_____

_____

_____

_____

PLANTING INSTRUCTION

_____

_____

_____

_____

ADDITIONAL NOTES

_____

_____

_____

_____

_____

_____

GARDENING LOGBOOK

NAME	LOCATION
SUPPLIER	PRICE

SCIENTIFIC CLASS

VEGETABLE	○	FRUIT
HERB	○	FLOWER
SHRUB	○	TREE
ANNUAL	○	BIENNIAL
PERENNIAL	○	SEEDLING

DATES

GERMINATED

PLANTED

HARVESTED

LIGHT LEVEL

SUN

PARTIAL SUN

SHADE

OTHER

STARTED FROM

SEED

PLANT

RATING

SIZE	○○○○○
COLOR	○○○○○
TASTE	○○○○○

FERTILIZERS & EQUIPMENT

_____

_____

_____

_____

_____

WATER REQUIREMENTS

0%
LESS

CARE INSTRUCTIONS

_____

_____

_____

_____

_____

PLANTING INSTRUCTION

_____

_____

_____

_____

ADDITIONAL NOTES

_____

_____

_____

_____

_____

_____

_____

GARDENING LOGBOOK

NAME	LOCATION
SUPPLIER	PRICE

SCIENTIFIC CLASS

- ○ VEGETABLE
- ○ HERB
- ○ SHRUB
- ○ ANNUAL
- ○ PERENNIAL

- FRUIT
- FLOWER
- TREE
- BIENNIAL
- SEEDLING

DATES

- GERMINATED
- PLANTED
- HARVESTED

LIGHT LEVEL

- SUN
- PARTIAL SUN
- SHADE
- OTHER

STARTED FROM

- SEED
- PLANT

RATING

- SIZE ○○○○○
- COLOR ○○○○○
- TASTE ○○○○○

FERTILIZERS & EQUIPMENT

_____

_____

_____

_____

_____

WATER REQUIREMENTS

0%
LESS

CARE INSTRUCTIONS

_____

_____

_____

_____

PLANTING INSTRUCTION

_____

_____

_____

_____

ADDITIONAL NOTES

_____

_____

_____

_____

_____

_____

_____

GARDENING LOGBOOK

NAME

LOCATION

SUPPLIER

PRICE

SCIENTIFIC CLASS

- VEGETABLE ○
- FRUIT
- HERB ○
- FLOWER
- SHRUB ○
- TREE
- ANNUAL ○
- BIENNIAL
- PERENNIAL ○
- SEEDLING

DATES

- GERMINATED
- PLANTED
- HARVESTED

LIGHT LEVEL

- SUN
- PARTIAL SUN
- SHADE
- OTHER

STARTED FROM

- SEED
- PLANT

RATING

- SIZE ○○○○○
- COLOR ○○○○○
- TASTE ○○○○○

FERTILIZERS & EQUIPMENT

_____

_____

_____

_____

_____

WATER REQUIREMENTS

0%
LESS

CARE INSTRUCTIONS

_____

_____

_____

_____

PLANTING INSTRUCTION

_____

_____

_____

_____

ADDITIONAL NOTES

_____

_____

_____

_____

_____

_____

GARDENING LOGBOOK

NAME	LOCATION
SUPPLIER	PRICE

SCIENTIFIC CLASS

- VEGETABLE ○
- HERB ○
- SHRUB ○
- ANNUAL ○
- PERENNIAL ○

- FRUIT
- FLOWER
- TREE
- BIENNIAL
- SEEDLING

DATES

GERMINATED

PLANTED

HARVESTED

LIGHT LEVEL

SUN

PARTIAL SUN

SHADE

OTHER

STARTED FROM

SEED

PLANT

RATING

SIZE ○○○○○

COLOR ○○○○○

TASTE ○○○○○

FERTILIZERS & EQUIPMENT

WATER REQUIREMENTS

0%
LESS

CARE INSTRUCTIONS

PLANTING INSTRUCTION

ADDITIONAL NOTES

GARDENING LOGBOOK

NAME	LOCATION
SUPPLIER	PRICE

SCIENTIFIC CLASS

- VEGETABLE ○
- HERB ○
- SHRUB ○
- ANNUAL ○
- PERENNIAL ○

- FRUIT
- FLOWER
- TREE
- BIENNIAL
- SEEDLING

DATES

- GERMINATED
- PLANTED
- HARVESTED

LIGHT LEVEL

- SUN
- PARTIAL SUN
- SHADE
- OTHER

STARTED FROM

- SEED
- PLANT

RATING

- SIZE ○○○○○
- COLOR ○○○○○
- TASTE ○○○○○

FERTILIZERS & EQUIPMENT

_____

_____

_____

_____

_____

WATER REQUIREMENTS

0%
LESS

CARE INSTRUCTIONS

_____

_____

_____

_____

_____

PLANTING INSTRUCTION

_____

_____

_____

_____

_____

ADDITIONAL NOTES

_____

_____

_____

_____

_____

_____

_____

GARDENING LOGBOOK

NAME		LOCATION	

SUPPLIER		PRICE	

SCIENTIFIC CLASS

VEGETABLE	○	FRUIT
HERB	○	FLOWER
SHRUB	○	TREE
ANNUAL	○	BIENNIAL
PERENNIAL	○	SEEDLING

DATES

GERMINATED

PLANTED

HARVESTED

LIGHT LEVEL

SUN

PARTIAL SUN

SHADE

OTHER

STARTED FROM

SEED

PLANT

RATING

SIZE	○○○○○
COLOR	○○○○○
TASTE	○○○○○

FERTILIZERS & EQUIPMENT

_____

_____

_____

_____

_____

WATER REQUIREMENTS

0%
LESS

CARE INSTRUCTIONS

_____

_____

_____

_____

PLANTING INSTRUCTION

_____

_____

_____

_____

ADDITIONAL NOTES

_____

_____

_____

_____

_____

_____

GARDENING LOGBOOK

NAME		LOCATION
SUPPLIER		PRICE

SCIENTIFIC CLASS

VEGETABLE	○	FRUIT
HERB	○	FLOWER
SHRUB	○	TREE
ANNUAL	○	BIENNIAL
PERENNIAL	○	SEEDLING

DATES

GERMINATED

PLANTED

HARVESTED

LIGHT LEVEL

SUN

PARTIAL SUN

SHADE

OTHER

STARTED FROM

SEED

PLANT

RATING

SIZE	○○○○○
COLOR	○○○○○
TASTE	○○○○○

FERTILIZERS & EQUIPMENT

_____

_____

_____

_____

_____

WATER REQUIREMENTS

0%
LESS ▭

CARE INSTRUCTIONS

_____

_____

_____

_____

PLANTING INSTRUCTION

_____

_____

_____

_____

ADDITIONAL NOTES

_____

_____

_____

_____

_____

_____

GARDENING LOGBOOK

NAME	LOCATION
SUPPLIER	PRICE

SCIENTIFIC CLASS

VEGETABLE	○	FRUIT
HERB	○	FLOWER
SHRUB	○	TREE
ANNUAL	○	BIENNIAL
PERENNIAL	○	SEEDLING

DATES

GERMINATED

PLANTED

HARVESTED

LIGHT LEVEL

SUN

PARTIAL SUN

SHADE

OTHER

STARTED FROM

SEED

PLANT

RATING

SIZE	○○○○○
COLOR	○○○○○
TASTE	○○○○○

FERTILIZERS & EQUIPMENT

WATER REQUIREMENTS

0%
LESS

CARE INSTRUCTIONS

PLANTING INSTRUCTION

ADDITIONAL NOTES

GARDENING LOGBOOK

NAME		LOCATION
SUPPLIER		PRICE

SCIENTIFIC CLASS

- VEGETABLE ○ FRUIT
- HERB ○ FLOWER
- SHRUB ○ TREE
- ANNUAL ○ BIENNIAL
- PERENNIAL ○ SEEDLING

DATES

GERMINATED

PLANTED

HARVESTED

STARTED FROM

SEED

PLANT

LIGHT LEVEL

SUN

PARTIAL SUN

SHADE

OTHER

RATING

SIZE ○○○○○

COLOR ○○○○○

TASTE ○○○○○

FERTILIZERS & EQUIPMENT

_____

_____

_____

_____

_____

WATER REQUIREMENTS

0%
LESS [_____]

CARE INSTRUCTIONS

_____

_____

_____

_____

PLANTING INSTRUCTION

_____

_____

_____

_____

ADDITIONAL NOTES

_____

_____

_____

_____

_____

_____

_____

GARDENING LOGBOOK

NAME	LOCATION
SUPPLIER	PRICE

SCIENTIFIC CLASS

VEGETABLE	○	FRUIT
HERB	○	FLOWER
SHRUB	○	TREE
ANNUAL	○	BIENNIAL
PERENNIAL	○	SEEDLING

DATES

GERMINATED

PLANTED

HARVESTED

LIGHT LEVEL

SUN

PARTIAL SUN

SHADE

OTHER

STARTED FROM

SEED

PLANT

RATING

SIZE	○○○○○
COLOR	○○○○○
TASTE	○○○○○

FERTILIZERS & EQUIPMENT

WATER REQUIREMENTS

0%
LESS

CARE INSTRUCTIONS

PLANTING INSTRUCTION

ADDITIONAL NOTES

GARDENING LOGBOOK

NAME	LOCATION
SUPPLIER	PRICE

SCIENTIFIC CLASS

- VEGETABLE ○
- FRUIT
- HERB ○
- FLOWER
- SHRUB ○
- TREE
- ANNUAL ○
- BIENNIAL
- PERENNIAL ○
- SEEDLING

DATES

GERMINATED

PLANTED

HARVESTED

LIGHT LEVEL

SUN

PARTIAL SUN

SHADE

OTHER

STARTED FROM

SEED

PLANT

RATING

SIZE ○○○○○

COLOR ○○○○○

TASTE ○○○○○

FERTILIZERS & EQUIPMENT

_____

_____

_____

_____

_____

WATER REQUIREMENTS

0%
LESS

CARE INSTRUCTIONS

_____

_____

_____

_____

_____

PLANTING INSTRUCTION

_____

_____

_____

_____

ADDITIONAL NOTES

_____

_____

_____

_____

_____

_____

_____

GARDENING LOGBOOK

NAME	LOCATION
SUPPLIER	PRICE

SCIENTIFIC CLASS

- VEGETABLE ○
- FRUIT
- HERB ○
- FLOWER
- SHRUB ○
- TREE
- ANNUAL ○
- BIENNIAL
- PERENNIAL ○
- SEEDLING

DATES

- GERMINATED
- PLANTED
- HARVESTED

LIGHT LEVEL

- SUN
- PARTIAL SUN
- SHADE
- OTHER

STARTED FROM

- SEED
- PLANT

RATING

- SIZE ○○○○○
- COLOR ○○○○○
- TASTE ○○○○○

FERTILIZERS & EQUIPMENT

_____

_____

_____

_____

_____

WATER REQUIREMENTS

0%
LESS

CARE INSTRUCTIONS

_____

_____

_____

_____

PLANTING INSTRUCTION

_____

_____

_____

_____

ADDITIONAL NOTES

_____

_____

_____

_____

_____

_____

_____

GARDENING LOGBOOK

NAME

LOCATION

SUPPLIER

PRICE

SCIENTIFIC CLASS

VEGETABLE ○	FRUIT
HERB ○	FLOWER
SHRUB ○	TREE
ANNUAL ○	BIENNIAL
PERENNIAL ○	SEEDLING

DATES

GERMINATED

PLANTED

HARVESTED

LIGHT LEVEL

SUN

PARTIAL SUN

SHADE

OTHER

STARTED FROM

SEED

PLANT

RATING

SIZE ○○○○○

COLOR ○○○○○

TASTE ○○○○○

FERTILIZERS & EQUIPMENT

_____

_____

_____

_____

_____

WATER REQUIREMENTS

0%
LESS

CARE INSTRUCTIONS

_____

_____

_____

_____

PLANTING INSTRUCTION

_____

_____

_____

_____

ADDITIONAL NOTES

_____

_____

_____

_____

_____

_____

_____

GARDENING LOGBOOK

NAME	LOCATION
SUPPLIER	PRICE

SCIENTIFIC CLASS

- VEGETABLE ○
- FRUIT
- HERB ○
- FLOWER
- SHRUB ○
- TREE
- ANNUAL ○
- BIENNIAL
- PERENNIAL ○
- SEEDLING

DATES

- GERMINATED
- PLANTED
- HARVESTED

LIGHT LEVEL

- SUN
- PARTIAL SUN
- SHADE
- OTHER

STARTED FROM

- SEED
- PLANT

RATING

- SIZE ○○○○○
- COLOR ○○○○○
- TASTE ○○○○○

FERTILIZERS & EQUIPMENT

WATER REQUIREMENTS

0%
LESS

CARE INSTRUCTIONS

PLANTING INSTRUCTION

ADDITIONAL NOTES

GARDENING LOGBOOK

NAME	LOCATION
SUPPLIER	PRICE

SCIENTIFIC CLASS

VEGETABLE ○	FRUIT
HERB ○	FLOWER
SHRUB ○	TREE
ANNUAL ○	BIENNIAL
PERENNIAL ○	SEEDLING

DATES

- GERMINATED
- PLANTED
- HARVESTED

LIGHT LEVEL

- SUN
- PARTIAL SUN
- SHADE
- OTHER

STARTED FROM

- SEED
- PLANT

RATING

SIZE	○○○○○
COLOR	○○○○○
TASTE	○○○○○

FERTILIZERS & EQUIPMENT

_____

_____

_____

_____

_____

WATER REQUIREMENTS

0%
LESS

CARE INSTRUCTIONS

_____

_____

_____

_____

PLANTING INSTRUCTION

_____

_____

_____

_____

ADDITIONAL NOTES

_____

_____

_____

_____

_____

_____

GARDENING LOGBOOK

NAME	LOCATION
SUPPLIER	PRICE

SCIENTIFIC CLASS

VEGETABLE	○	FRUIT
HERB	○	FLOWER
SHRUB	○	TREE
ANNUAL	○	BIENNIAL
PERENNIAL	○	SEEDLING

DATES

- GERMINATED
- PLANTED
- HARVESTED

LIGHT LEVEL

- SUN
- PARTIAL SUN
- SHADE
- OTHER

STARTED FROM

- SEED
- PLANT

RATING

SIZE	○○○○○
COLOR	○○○○○
TASTE	○○○○○

FERTILIZERS & EQUIPMENT

_____

_____

_____

_____

_____

WATER REQUIREMENTS

0%
LESS ▭

CARE INSTRUCTIONS

_____

_____

_____

_____

PLANTING INSTRUCTION

_____

_____

_____

_____

ADDITIONAL NOTES

_____

_____

_____

_____

_____

_____

_____

GARDENING LOGBOOK

NAME	LOCATION
SUPPLIER	PRICE

SCIENTIFIC CLASS

VEGETABLE	○	FRUIT
HERB	○	FLOWER
SHRUB	○	TREE
ANNUAL	○	BIENNIAL
PERENNIAL	○	SEEDLING

DATES

- GERMINATED
- PLANTED
- HARVESTED

LIGHT LEVEL

- SUN
- PARTIAL SUN
- SHADE
- OTHER

STARTED FROM

- SEED
- PLANT

RATING

SIZE	○○○○○
COLOR	○○○○○
TASTE	○○○○○

FERTILIZERS & EQUIPMENT

WATER REQUIREMENTS

0%
LESS

CARE INSTRUCTIONS

PLANTING INSTRUCTION

ADDITIONAL NOTES

GARDENING LOGBOOK

NAME		LOCATION
SUPPLIER		PRICE

SCIENTIFIC CLASS

- VEGETABLE ○
- FRUIT
- HERB ○
- FLOWER
- SHRUB ○
- TREE
- ANNUAL ○
- BIENNIAL
- PERENNIAL ○
- SEEDLING

DATES

- GERMINATED
- PLANTED
- HARVESTED

LIGHT LEVEL

- SUN
- PARTIAL SUN
- SHADE
- OTHER

STARTED FROM

- SEED
- PLANT

RATING

- SIZE ○○○○○
- COLOR ○○○○○
- TASTE ○○○○○

FERTILIZERS & EQUIPMENT

_____

_____

_____

_____

_____

WATER REQUIREMENTS

0%
LESS

CARE INSTRUCTIONS

_____

_____

_____

_____

PLANTING INSTRUCTION

_____

_____

_____

_____

ADDITIONAL NOTES

_____

_____

_____

_____

_____

_____

_____

GARDENING LOGBOOK

NAME	LOCATION
SUPPLIER	PRICE

SCIENTIFIC CLASS

VEGETABLE	○	FRUIT
HERB	○	FLOWER
SHRUB	○	TREE
ANNUAL	○	BIENNIAL
PERENNIAL	○	SEEDLING

DATES

GERMINATED

PLANTED

HARVESTED

LIGHT LEVEL

SUN

PARTIAL SUN

SHADE

OTHER

STARTED FROM

SEED

PLANT

RATING

SIZE	○○○○○
COLOR	○○○○○
TASTE	○○○○○

FERTILIZERS & EQUIPMENT

WATER REQUIREMENTS

0%
LESS

CARE INSTRUCTIONS

PLANTING INSTRUCTION

ADDITIONAL NOTES

GARDENING LOGBOOK

NAME	LOCATION
SUPPLIER	PRICE

SCIENTIFIC CLASS

VEGETABLE ○	FRUIT
HERB ○	FLOWER
SHRUB ○	TREE
ANNUAL ○	BIENNIAL
PERENNIAL ○	SEEDLING

DATES

GERMINATED

PLANTED

HARVESTED

LIGHT LEVEL

SUN

PARTIAL SUN

SHADE

OTHER

STARTED FROM

SEED

PLANT

RATING

SIZE ○○○○○

COLOR ○○○○○

TASTE ○○○○○

FERTILIZERS & EQUIPMENT

WATER REQUIREMENTS

0%
LESS

CARE INSTRUCTIONS

PLANTING INSTRUCTION

ADDITIONAL NOTES

GARDENING LOGBOOK

NAME	LOCATION
SUPPLIER	PRICE

SCIENTIFIC CLASS

- VEGETABLE ○
- FRUIT
- HERB ○
- FLOWER
- SHRUB ○
- TREE
- ANNUAL ○
- BIENNIAL
- PERENNIAL ○
- SEEDLING

DATES

- GERMINATED
- PLANTED
- HARVESTED

LIGHT LEVEL

- SUN
- PARTIAL SUN
- SHADE
- OTHER

STARTED FROM

- SEED
- PLANT

RATING

- SIZE ○○○○○
- COLOR ○○○○○
- TASTE ○○○○○

FERTILIZERS & EQUIPMENT

_____

_____

_____

_____

_____

WATER REQUIREMENTS

0%
LESS

CARE INSTRUCTIONS

_____

_____

_____

_____

PLANTING INSTRUCTION

_____

_____

_____

_____

ADDITIONAL NOTES

_____

_____

_____

_____

_____

_____

GARDENING LOGBOOK

NAME	LOCATION
SUPPLIER	PRICE

SCIENTIFIC CLASS

- ○ VEGETABLE
- ○ FRUIT
- ○ HERB
- ○ FLOWER
- ○ SHRUB
- ○ TREE
- ○ ANNUAL
- ○ BIENNIAL
- ○ PERENNIAL
- ○ SEEDLING

DATES

- GERMINATED
- PLANTED
- HARVESTED

LIGHT LEVEL

- SUN
- PARTIAL SUN
- SHADE
- OTHER

STARTED FROM

- SEED
- PLANT

RATING

- SIZE ○○○○○
- COLOR ○○○○○
- TASTE ○○○○○

FERTILIZERS & EQUIPMENT

_____

_____

_____

_____

_____

WATER REQUIREMENTS

0%
LESS ☐

CARE INSTRUCTIONS

_____

_____

_____

_____

_____

PLANTING INSTRUCTION

_____

_____

_____

_____

ADDITIONAL NOTES

_____

_____

_____

_____

_____

_____

_____

_____

GARDENING LOGBOOK

NAME	LOCATION
SUPPLIER	PRICE

SCIENTIFIC CLASS

VEGETABLE ○	FRUIT
HERB ○	FLOWER
SHRUB ○	TREE
ANNUAL ○	BIENNIAL
PERENNIAL ○	SEEDLING

DATES

GERMINATED

PLANTED

HARVESTED

LIGHT LEVEL

SUN

PARTIAL SUN

SHADE

OTHER

STARTED FROM

SEED

PLANT

RATING

SIZE	○○○○○
COLOR	○○○○○
TASTE	○○○○○

FERTILIZERS & EQUIPMENT

_____

_____

_____

_____

_____

WATER REQUIREMENTS

0%
LESS

CARE INSTRUCTIONS

_____

_____

_____

_____

PLANTING INSTRUCTION

_____

_____

_____

_____

ADDITIONAL NOTES

_____

_____

_____

_____

_____

_____

_____

GARDENING LOGBOOK

NAME	LOCATION
SUPPLIER	PRICE

SCIENTIFIC CLASS

VEGETABLE ○	FRUIT
HERB ○	FLOWER
SHRUB ○	TREE
ANNUAL ○	BIENNIAL
PERENNIAL ○	SEEDLING

DATES

GERMINATED

PLANTED

HARVESTED

LIGHT LEVEL

SUN

PARTIAL SUN

SHADE

OTHER

STARTED FROM

SEED

PLANT

RATING

SIZE	○○○○○
COLOR	○○○○○
TASTE	○○○○○

FERTILIZERS & EQUIPMENT

_____

_____

_____

_____

_____

WATER REQUIREMENTS

0%
LESS

CARE INSTRUCTIONS

_____

_____

_____

_____

PLANTING INSTRUCTION

_____

_____

_____

_____

ADDITIONAL NOTES

_____

_____

_____

_____

_____

_____

GARDENING LOGBOOK

NAME	LOCATION
SUPPLIER	PRICE

SCIENTIFIC CLASS

VEGETABLE ○	FRUIT
HERB ○	FLOWER
SHRUB ○	TREE
ANNUAL ○	BIENNIAL
PERENNIAL ○	SEEDLING

DATES

GERMINATED

PLANTED

HARVESTED

LIGHT LEVEL

SUN

PARTIAL SUN

SHADE

OTHER

STARTED FROM

SEED

PLANT

RATING

SIZE ○○○○○

COLOR ○○○○○

TASTE ○○○○○

FERTILIZERS & EQUIPMENT

_____

_____

_____

_____

_____

WATER REQUIREMENTS

0%
LESS

CARE INSTRUCTIONS

_____

_____

_____

_____

_____

PLANTING INSTRUCTION

_____

_____

_____

_____

ADDITIONAL NOTES

_____

_____

_____

_____

_____

_____

_____

GARDENING LOGBOOK

NAME	LOCATION
SUPPLIER	PRICE

SCIENTIFIC CLASS

VEGETABLE	○	FRUIT	
HERB	○	FLOWER	
SHRUB	○	TREE	
ANNUAL	○	BIENNIAL	
PERENNIAL	○	SEEDLING	

DATES

GERMINATED _____

PLANTED _____

HARVESTED _____

LIGHT LEVEL

SUN

PARTIAL SUN

SHADE

OTHER

STARTED FROM

SEED _____

PLANT _____

_____

RATING

SIZE	○○○○○
COLOR	○○○○○
TASTE	○○○○○

FERTILIZERS & EQUIPMENT

WATER REQUIREMENTS

0%
LESS

CARE INSTRUCTIONS

PLANTING INSTRUCTION

ADDITIONAL NOTES

GARDENING LOGBOOK

NAME		LOCATION
SUPPLIER		PRICE

SCIENTIFIC CLASS

VEGETABLE	○	FRUIT
HERB	○	FLOWER
SHRUB	○	TREE
ANNUAL	○	BIENNIAL
PERENNIAL	○	SEEDLING

DATES

GERMINATED

PLANTED

HARVESTED

LIGHT LEVEL

SUN

PARTIAL SUN

SHADE

OTHER

STARTED FROM

SEED

PLANT

RATING

SIZE	○○○○○
COLOR	○○○○○
TASTE	○○○○○

FERTILIZERS & EQUIPMENT

_____

_____

_____

_____

_____

WATER REQUIREMENTS

0%
LESS

CARE INSTRUCTIONS

_____

_____

_____

_____

PLANTING INSTRUCTION

_____

_____

_____

_____

ADDITIONAL NOTES

_____

_____

_____

_____

_____

_____

GARDENING LOGBOOK

NAME	LOCATION
SUPPLIER	PRICE

SCIENTIFIC CLASS

VEGETABLE	○	FRUIT
HERB	○	FLOWER
SHRUB	○	TREE
ANNUAL	○	BIENNIAL
PERENNIAL	○	SEEDLING

DATES

GERMINATED

PLANTED

HARVESTED

LIGHT LEVEL

SUN

PARTIAL SUN

SHADE

OTHER

STARTED FROM

SEED

PLANT

RATING

SIZE	○○○○○
COLOR	○○○○○
TASTE	○○○○○

FERTILIZERS & EQUIPMENT

WATER REQUIREMENTS

0%
LESS

CARE INSTRUCTIONS

PLANTING INSTRUCTION

ADDITIONAL NOTES

GARDENING LOGBOOK

NAME	LOCATION
SUPPLIER	PRICE

SCIENTIFIC CLASS

- ○ VEGETABLE
- ○ HERB
- ○ SHRUB
- ○ ANNUAL
- ○ PERENNIAL

- FRUIT
- FLOWER
- TREE
- BIENNIAL
- SEEDLING

DATES

- GERMINATED
- PLANTED
- HARVESTED

STARTED FROM

- SEED
- PLANT

LIGHT LEVEL

- SUN
- PARTIAL SUN
- SHADE
- OTHER

RATING

- SIZE ○○○○○
- COLOR ○○○○○
- TASTE ○○○○○

FERTILIZERS & EQUIPMENT

_____

_____

_____

_____

_____

WATER REQUIREMENTS

0%
LESS

CARE INSTRUCTIONS

_____

_____

_____

_____

_____

PLANTING INSTRUCTION

_____

_____

_____

_____

ADDITIONAL NOTES

_____

_____

_____

_____

_____

_____

_____

_____

GARDENING LOGBOOK

NAME	LOCATION
SUPPLIER	PRICE

SCIENTIFIC CLASS

VEGETABLE	○	FRUIT
HERB	○	FLOWER
SHRUB	○	TREE
ANNUAL	○	BIENNIAL
PERENNIAL	○	SEEDLING

DATES

GERMINATED

PLANTED

HARVESTED

LIGHT LEVEL

SUN

PARTIAL SUN

SHADE

OTHER

STARTED FROM

SEED

PLANT

RATING

SIZE	○○○○○
COLOR	○○○○○
TASTE	○○○○○

FERTILIZERS & EQUIPMENT

_____

_____

_____

_____

_____

WATER REQUIREMENTS

0%
LESS

CARE INSTRUCTIONS

_____

_____

_____

_____

PLANTING INSTRUCTION

_____

_____

_____

_____

ADDITIONAL NOTES

_____

_____

_____

_____

_____

_____

GARDENING LOGBOOK

NAME	LOCATION
SUPPLIER	PRICE

SCIENTIFIC CLASS

VEGETABLE ○	FRUIT
HERB ○	FLOWER
SHRUB ○	TREE
ANNUAL ○	BIENNIAL
PERENNIAL ○	SEEDLING

DATES

GERMINATED

PLANTED

HARVESTED

LIGHT LEVEL

SUN

PARTIAL SUN

SHADE

OTHER

STARTED FROM

SEED

PLANT

RATING

SIZE	○○○○○
COLOR	○○○○○
TASTE	○○○○○

FERTILIZERS & EQUIPMENT

WATER REQUIREMENTS

0%
LESS

CARE INSTRUCTIONS

PLANTING INSTRUCTION

ADDITIONAL NOTES

GARDENING LOGBOOK

NAME	LOCATION
SUPPLIER	PRICE

SCIENTIFIC CLASS

- ○ VEGETABLE — FRUIT
- ○ HERB — FLOWER
- ○ SHRUB — TREE
- ○ ANNUAL — BIENNIAL
- ○ PERENNIAL — SEEDLING

DATES

- GERMINATED
- PLANTED
- HARVESTED

LIGHT LEVEL

- SUN
- PARTIAL SUN
- SHADE
- OTHER

STARTED FROM

- SEED
- PLANT

RATING

- SIZE ○○○○○
- COLOR ○○○○○
- TASTE ○○○○○

FERTILIZERS & EQUIPMENT

_____

_____

_____

_____

_____

WATER REQUIREMENTS

0%
LESS

CARE INSTRUCTIONS

_____

_____

_____

_____

_____

PLANTING INSTRUCTION

_____

_____

_____

_____

ADDITIONAL NOTES

_____

_____

_____

_____

_____

_____

_____

GARDENING LOGBOOK

NAME		LOCATION

SUPPLIER		PRICE

SCIENTIFIC CLASS

- VEGETABLE ○
- FRUIT
- HERB ○
- FLOWER
- SHRUB ○
- TREE
- ANNUAL ○
- BIENNIAL
- PERENNIAL ○
- SEEDLING

DATES

- GERMINATED
- PLANTED
- HARVESTED

LIGHT LEVEL

- SUN
- PARTIAL SUN
- SHADE
- OTHER

STARTED FROM

- SEED
- PLANT

RATING

- SIZE ○○○○○
- COLOR ○○○○○
- TASTE ○○○○○

FERTILIZERS & EQUIPMENT

_____

_____

_____

_____

_____

WATER REQUIREMENTS

0%
LESS

CARE INSTRUCTIONS

_____

_____

_____

_____

PLANTING INSTRUCTION

_____

_____

_____

_____

ADDITIONAL NOTES

_____

_____

_____

_____

_____

_____

GARDENING LOGBOOK

NAME	LOCATION
SUPPLIER	PRICE

SCIENTIFIC CLASS

VEGETABLE	○	FRUIT
HERB	○	FLOWER
SHRUB	○	TREE
ANNUAL	○	BIENNIAL
PERENNIAL	○	SEEDLING

DATES

GERMINATED

PLANTED

HARVESTED

LIGHT LEVEL

SUN

PARTIAL SUN

SHADE

OTHER

STARTED FROM

SEED

PLANT

RATING

SIZE ○○○○○

COLOR ○○○○○

TASTE ○○○○○

FERTILIZERS & EQUIPMENT

WATER REQUIREMENTS

0%
LESS

CARE INSTRUCTIONS

PLANTING INSTRUCTION

ADDITIONAL NOTES

GARDENING LOGBOOK

NAME		LOCATION
SUPPLIER		PRICE

SCIENTIFIC CLASS

VEGETABLE	○	FRUIT
HERB	○	FLOWER
SHRUB	○	TREE
ANNUAL	○	BIENNIAL
PERENNIAL	○	SEEDLING

DATES

GERMINATED

PLANTED

HARVESTED

LIGHT LEVEL

SUN

PARTIAL SUN

SHADE

OTHER

STARTED FROM

SEED

PLANT

RATING

SIZE	○○○○○
COLOR	○○○○○
TASTE	○○○○○

FERTILIZERS & EQUIPMENT

_____

_____

_____

_____

_____

WATER REQUIREMENTS

0%
LESS

CARE INSTRUCTIONS

_____

_____

_____

_____

_____

PLANTING INSTRUCTION

_____

_____

_____

_____

_____

ADDITIONAL NOTES

_____

_____

_____

_____

_____

_____

_____

GARDENING LOGBOOK

NAME		LOCATION
SUPPLIER		PRICE

SCIENTIFIC CLASS

- VEGETABLE ○ FRUIT
- HERB ○ FLOWER
- SHRUB ○ TREE
- ANNUAL ○ BIENNIAL
- PERENNIAL ○ SEEDLING

DATES

- GERMINATED
- PLANTED
- HARVESTED

LIGHT LEVEL

- SUN
- PARTIAL SUN
- SHADE
- OTHER

STARTED FROM

- SEED
- PLANT

RATING

- SIZE ○○○○○
- COLOR ○○○○○
- TASTE ○○○○○

FERTILIZERS & EQUIPMENT

WATER REQUIREMENTS

0%
LESS

CARE INSTRUCTIONS

PLANTING INSTRUCTION

ADDITIONAL NOTES

GARDENING LOGBOOK

NAME	LOCATION
SUPPLIER	PRICE

SCIENTIFIC CLASS

VEGETABLE ○	FRUIT
HERB ○	FLOWER
SHRUB ○	TREE
ANNUAL ○	BIENNIAL
PERENNIAL ○	SEEDLING

DATES

GERMINATED

PLANTED

HARVESTED

LIGHT LEVEL

SUN

PARTIAL SUN

SHADE

OTHER

STARTED FROM

SEED

PLANT

RATING

SIZE ○○○○○

COLOR ○○○○○

TASTE ○○○○○

FERTILIZERS & EQUIPMENT

_____

_____

_____

_____

_____

WATER REQUIREMENTS

0%
LESS

CARE INSTRUCTIONS

_____

_____

_____

_____

PLANTING INSTRUCTION

_____

_____

_____

_____

ADDITIONAL NOTES

_____

_____

_____

_____

_____

_____

_____

GARDENING LOGBOOK

NAME	LOCATION
SUPPLIER	PRICE

SCIENTIFIC CLASS

- VEGETABLE ○
- HERB ○
- SHRUB ○
- ANNUAL ○
- PERENNIAL ○

- FRUIT
- FLOWER
- TREE
- BIENNIAL
- SEEDLING

DATES

- GERMINATED
- PLANTED
- HARVESTED

LIGHT LEVEL

- SUN
- PARTIAL SUN
- SHADE
- OTHER

STARTED FROM

- SEED
- PLANT

RATING

- SIZE ○○○○○
- COLOR ○○○○○
- TASTE ○○○○○

FERTILIZERS & EQUIPMENT

_____

_____

_____

_____

WATER REQUIREMENTS

0%
LESS

CARE INSTRUCTIONS

_____

_____

_____

_____

PLANTING INSTRUCTION

_____

_____

_____

_____

ADDITIONAL NOTES

_____

_____

_____

_____

_____

_____

_____

GARDENING LOGBOOK

NAME	LOCATION
SUPPLIER	PRICE

SCIENTIFIC CLASS

VEGETABLE	○	FRUIT
HERB	○	FLOWER
SHRUB	○	TREE
ANNUAL	○	BIENNIAL
PERENNIAL	○	SEEDLING

DATES

GERMINATED

PLANTED

HARVESTED

LIGHT LEVEL

SUN

PARTIAL SUN

SHADE

OTHER

STARTED FROM

SEED

PLANT

RATING

SIZE	○○○○○
COLOR	○○○○○
TASTE	○○○○○

FERTILIZERS & EQUIPMENT

_____

_____

_____

_____

_____

WATER REQUIREMENTS

0%
LESS

CARE INSTRUCTIONS

_____

_____

_____

_____

PLANTING INSTRUCTION

_____

_____

_____

_____

ADDITIONAL NOTES

_____

_____

_____

_____

_____

_____

GARDENING LOGBOOK

NAME	LOCATION
SUPPLIER	PRICE

SCIENTIFIC CLASS

VEGETABLE ○	FRUIT
HERB ○	FLOWER
SHRUB ○	TREE
ANNUAL ○	BIENNIAL
PERENNIAL ○	SEEDLING

DATES

- GERMINATED
- PLANTED
- HARVESTED

LIGHT LEVEL

- SUN
- PARTIAL SUN
- SHADE
- OTHER

STARTED FROM

- SEED
- PLANT

RATING

SIZE	○○○○○
COLOR	○○○○○
TASTE	○○○○○

FERTILIZERS & EQUIPMENT

_____

_____

_____

_____

_____

WATER REQUIREMENTS

0%
LESS

CARE INSTRUCTIONS

_____

_____

_____

_____

PLANTING INSTRUCTION

_____

_____

_____

_____

ADDITIONAL NOTES

_____

_____

_____

_____

_____

_____

GARDENING LOGBOOK

NAME		LOCATION

SUPPLIER		PRICE

SCIENTIFIC CLASS

- ○ VEGETABLE
- ○ FRUIT
- ○ HERB
- ○ FLOWER
- ○ SHRUB
- ○ TREE
- ○ ANNUAL
- ○ BIENNIAL
- ○ PERENNIAL
- ○ SEEDLING

DATES

- GERMINATED
- PLANTED
- HARVESTED

LIGHT LEVEL

- SUN
- PARTIAL SUN
- SHADE
- OTHER

STARTED FROM

- SEED
- PLANT

RATING

- SIZE   ○○○○○
- COLOR   ○○○○○
- TASTE   ○○○○○

FERTILIZERS & EQUIPMENT

_____

_____

_____

_____

_____

WATER REQUIREMENTS

0%
LESS

CARE INSTRUCTIONS

_____

_____

_____

_____

_____

PLANTING INSTRUCTION

_____

_____

_____

_____

ADDITIONAL NOTES

_____

_____

_____

_____

_____

_____

_____

GARDENING LOGBOOK

NAME	LOCATION
SUPPLIER	PRICE

SCIENTIFIC CLASS

- VEGETABLE ○   FRUIT
- HERB ○   FLOWER
- SHRUB ○   TREE
- ANNUAL ○   BIENNIAL
- PERENNIAL ○   SEEDLING

DATES

- GERMINATED
- PLANTED
- HARVESTED

LIGHT LEVEL

- SUN
- PARTIAL SUN
- SHADE
- OTHER

STARTED FROM

- SEED
- PLANT

RATING

- SIZE   ○○○○○
- COLOR   ○○○○○
- TASTE   ○○○○○

FERTILIZERS & EQUIPMENT

_____

_____

_____

_____

_____

WATER REQUIREMENTS

0%
LESS

CARE INSTRUCTIONS

_____

_____

_____

_____

PLANTING INSTRUCTION

_____

_____

_____

_____

ADDITIONAL NOTES

_____

_____

_____

_____

_____

_____

GARDENING LOGBOOK

NAME	LOCATION
SUPPLIER	PRICE

SCIENTIFIC CLASS

VEGETABLE	○	FRUIT
HERB	○	FLOWER
SHRUB	○	TREE
ANNUAL	○	BIENNIAL
PERENNIAL	○	SEEDLING

DATES

GERMINATED

PLANTED

HARVESTED

LIGHT LEVEL

SUN

PARTIAL SUN

SHADE

OTHER

STARTED FROM

SEED

PLANT

RATING

SIZE	○○○○○
COLOR	○○○○○
TASTE	○○○○○

FERTILIZERS & EQUIPMENT

_____

_____

_____

_____

_____

WATER REQUIREMENTS

0%
LESS

CARE INSTRUCTIONS

_____

_____

_____

_____

PLANTING INSTRUCTION

_____

_____

_____

_____

ADDITIONAL NOTES

_____

_____

_____

_____

_____

_____

_____

GARDENING LOGBOOK

NAME	LOCATION
SUPPLIER	PRICE

SCIENTIFIC CLASS

VEGETABLE ○	FRUIT
HERB ○	FLOWER
SHRUB ○	TREE
ANNUAL ○	BIENNIAL
PERENNIAL ○	SEEDLING

DATES

- GERMINATED
- PLANTED
- HARVESTED

LIGHT LEVEL

- SUN
- PARTIAL SUN
- SHADE
- OTHER

STARTED FROM

- SEED
- PLANT

RATING

SIZE	○○○○○
COLOR	○○○○○
TASTE	○○○○○

FERTILIZERS & EQUIPMENT

_____

_____

_____

_____

_____

WATER REQUIREMENTS

0%
LESS

CARE INSTRUCTIONS

_____

_____

_____

_____

PLANTING INSTRUCTION

_____

_____

_____

_____

ADDITIONAL NOTES

_____

_____

_____

_____

_____

_____

_____

GARDENING LOGBOOK

NAME	LOCATION
SUPPLIER	PRICE

SCIENTIFIC CLASS

- VEGETABLE ○ FRUIT
- HERB ○ FLOWER
- SHRUB ○ TREE
- ANNUAL ○ BIENNIAL
- PERENNIAL ○ SEEDLING

DATES

- GERMINATED
- PLANTED
- HARVESTED

LIGHT LEVEL

- SUN
- PARTIAL SUN
- SHADE
- OTHER

STARTED FROM

- SEED
- PLANT

RATING

- SIZE ○○○○○
- COLOR ○○○○○
- TASTE ○○○○○

FERTILIZERS & EQUIPMENT

_____

_____

_____

_____

_____

WATER REQUIREMENTS

0%
LESS

CARE INSTRUCTIONS

_____

_____

_____

_____

_____

PLANTING INSTRUCTION

_____

_____

_____

_____

_____

ADDITIONAL NOTES

_____

_____

_____

_____

_____

_____

_____

GARDENING LOGBOOK

NAME		LOCATION
SUPPLIER		PRICE

SCIENTIFIC CLASS

VEGETABLE	○	FRUIT
HERB	○	FLOWER
SHRUB	○	TREE
ANNUAL	○	BIENNIAL
PERENNIAL	○	SEEDLING

DATES

GERMINATED

PLANTED

HARVESTED

LIGHT LEVEL

SUN

PARTIAL SUN

SHADE

OTHER

STARTED FROM

SEED

PLANT

RATING

SIZE	○○○○○
COLOR	○○○○○
TASTE	○○○○○

FERTILIZERS & EQUIPMENT

_____

_____

_____

_____

_____

WATER REQUIREMENTS

0%
LESS

CARE INSTRUCTIONS

_____

_____

_____

_____

_____

PLANTING INSTRUCTION

_____

_____

_____

_____

ADDITIONAL NOTES

_____

_____

_____

_____

_____

_____

_____

GARDENING LOGBOOK

NAME	LOCATION
SUPPLIER	PRICE

SCIENTIFIC CLASS

VEGETABLE	○	FRUIT
HERB	○	FLOWER
SHRUB	○	TREE
ANNUAL	○	BIENNIAL
PERENNIAL	○	SEEDLING

DATES

GERMINATED

PLANTED

HARVESTED

LIGHT LEVEL

SUN

PARTIAL SUN

SHADE

OTHER

STARTED FROM

SEED

PLANT

RATING

SIZE	○○○○○
COLOR	○○○○○
TASTE	○○○○○

FERTILIZERS & EQUIPMENT

WATER REQUIREMENTS

0%
LESS

CARE INSTRUCTIONS

PLANTING INSTRUCTION

ADDITIONAL NOTES

GARDENING LOGBOOK

NAME		LOCATION

SUPPLIER		PRICE

SCIENTIFIC CLASS

VEGETABLE	○	FRUIT
HERB	○	FLOWER
SHRUB	○	TREE
ANNUAL	○	BIENNIAL
PERENNIAL	○	SEEDLING

DATES

GERMINATED

PLANTED

HARVESTED

LIGHT LEVEL

SUN

PARTIAL SUN

SHADE

OTHER

STARTED FROM

SEED

PLANT

RATING

SIZE	○○○○○
COLOR	○○○○○
TASTE	○○○○○

FERTILIZERS & EQUIPMENT

_____

_____

_____

_____

_____

WATER REQUIREMENTS

0%
LESS

CARE INSTRUCTIONS

_____

_____

_____

_____

PLANTING INSTRUCTION

_____

_____

_____

_____

ADDITIONAL NOTES

_____

_____

_____

_____

_____

_____

_____

GARDENING LOGBOOK

NAME	LOCATION
SUPPLIER	PRICE

SCIENTIFIC CLASS

VEGETABLE ○	FRUIT
HERB ○	FLOWER
SHRUB ○	TREE
ANNUAL ○	BIENNIAL
PERENNIAL ○	SEEDLING

DATES

GERMINATED

PLANTED

HARVESTED

LIGHT LEVEL

SUN

PARTIAL SUN

SHADE

OTHER

STARTED FROM

SEED

PLANT

RATING

SIZE ○○○○○

COLOR ○○○○○

TASTE ○○○○○

FERTILIZERS & EQUIPMENT

_____

_____

_____

_____

_____

WATER REQUIREMENTS

0%
LESS

CARE INSTRUCTIONS

_____

_____

_____

_____

_____

PLANTING INSTRUCTION

_____

_____

_____

_____

ADDITIONAL NOTES

_____

_____

_____

_____

_____

_____

_____

GARDENING LOGBOOK

NAME		LOCATION

SUPPLIER		PRICE

SCIENTIFIC CLASS

VEGETABLE	○	FRUIT
HERB	○	FLOWER
SHRUB	○	TREE
ANNUAL	○	BIENNIAL
PERENNIAL	○	SEEDLING

DATES

GERMINATED

PLANTED

HARVESTED

LIGHT LEVEL

SUN

PARTIAL SUN

SHADE

OTHER

STARTED FROM

SEED

PLANT

RATING

SIZE ○○○○○

COLOR ○○○○○

TASTE ○○○○○

FERTILIZERS & EQUIPMENT

WATER REQUIREMENTS

0%
LESS

CARE INSTRUCTIONS

PLANTING INSTRUCTION

ADDITIONAL NOTES

GARDENING LOGBOOK

NAME	LOCATION
SUPPLIER	PRICE

SCIENTIFIC CLASS

- VEGETABLE ○
- FRUIT
- HERB ○
- FLOWER
- SHRUB ○
- TREE
- ANNUAL ○
- BIENNIAL
- PERENNIAL ○
- SEEDLING

DATES

GERMINATED

PLANTED

HARVESTED

LIGHT LEVEL

SUN

PARTIAL SUN

SHADE

OTHER

STARTED FROM

SEED

PLANT

RATING

SIZE ○○○○○

COLOR ○○○○○

TASTE ○○○○○

FERTILIZERS & EQUIPMENT

_____

_____

_____

_____

_____

WATER REQUIREMENTS

0%
LESS

CARE INSTRUCTIONS

_____

_____

_____

_____

PLANTING INSTRUCTION

_____

_____

_____

_____

ADDITIONAL NOTES

_____

_____

_____

_____

_____

_____

GARDENING LOGBOOK

NAME

LOCATION

SUPPLIER

PRICE

SCIENTIFIC CLASS

VEGETABLE	○	FRUIT
HERB	○	FLOWER
SHRUB	○	TREE
ANNUAL	○	BIENNIAL
PERENNIAL	○	SEEDLING

DATES

GERMINATED

PLANTED

HARVESTED

LIGHT LEVEL

SUN

PARTIAL SUN

SHADE

OTHER

STARTED FROM

SEED

PLANT

RATING

SIZE ○○○○○

COLOR ○○○○○

TASTE ○○○○○

FERTILIZERS & EQUIPMENT

_____

_____

_____

_____

WATER REQUIREMENTS

0%
LESS

CARE INSTRUCTIONS

_____

_____

_____

_____

_____

PLANTING INSTRUCTION

_____

_____

_____

_____

ADDITIONAL NOTES

_____

_____

_____

_____

_____

_____

_____

GARDENING LOGBOOK

NAME	LOCATION
SUPPLIER	PRICE

SCIENTIFIC CLASS

VEGETABLE	○	FRUIT
HERB	○	FLOWER
SHRUB	○	TREE
ANNUAL	○	BIENNIAL
PERENNIAL	○	SEEDLING

DATES

GERMINATED

PLANTED

HARVESTED

LIGHT LEVEL

SUN

PARTIAL SUN

SHADE

OTHER

STARTED FROM

SEED

PLANT

RATING

SIZE	○○○○○
COLOR	○○○○○
TASTE	○○○○○

FERTILIZERS & EQUIPMENT

_____

_____

_____

_____

_____

WATER REQUIREMENTS

0%
LESS

CARE INSTRUCTIONS

_____

_____

_____

_____

_____

PLANTING INSTRUCTION

_____

_____

_____

_____

ADDITIONAL NOTES

_____

_____

_____

_____

_____

_____

_____

GARDENING LOGBOOK

NAME		LOCATION
SUPPLIER		PRICE

SCIENTIFIC CLASS

VEGETABLE	○	FRUIT
HERB	○	FLOWER
SHRUB	○	TREE
ANNUAL	○	BIENNIAL
PERENNIAL	○	SEEDLING

DATES

GERMINATED

PLANTED

HARVESTED

LIGHT LEVEL

SUN

PARTIAL SUN

SHADE

OTHER

STARTED FROM

SEED

PLANT

RATING

SIZE	○○○○○
COLOR	○○○○○
TASTE	○○○○○

FERTILIZERS & EQUIPMENT

_____

_____

_____

_____

_____

WATER REQUIREMENTS

0%
LESS

CARE INSTRUCTIONS

_____

_____

_____

_____

PLANTING INSTRUCTION

_____

_____

_____

_____

ADDITIONAL NOTES

_____

_____

_____

_____

_____

_____

GARDENING LOGBOOK

NAME	LOCATION
SUPPLIER	PRICE

SCIENTIFIC CLASS

- ○ VEGETABLE
- ○ HERB
- ○ SHRUB
- ○ ANNUAL
- ○ PERENNIAL

- FRUIT
- FLOWER
- TREE
- BIENNIAL
- SEEDLING

DATES

GERMINATED

PLANTED

HARVESTED

LIGHT LEVEL

SUN

PARTIAL SUN

SHADE

OTHER

STARTED FROM

SEED

PLANT

RATING

SIZE ○○○○○

COLOR ○○○○○

TASTE ○○○○○

FERTILIZERS & EQUIPMENT

_____

_____

_____

_____

_____

WATER REQUIREMENTS

0%
LESS

CARE INSTRUCTIONS

_____

_____

_____

_____

PLANTING INSTRUCTION

_____

_____

_____

_____

ADDITIONAL NOTES

_____

_____

_____

_____

_____

_____

_____

GARDENING LOGBOOK

NAME	LOCATION
SUPPLIER	PRICE

SCIENTIFIC CLASS

VEGETABLE	○	FRUIT
HERB	○	FLOWER
SHRUB	○	TREE
ANNUAL	○	BIENNIAL
PERENNIAL	○	SEEDLING

DATES

GERMINATED

PLANTED

HARVESTED

LIGHT LEVEL

SUN

PARTIAL SUN

SHADE

OTHER

STARTED FROM

SEED

PLANT

RATING

SIZE	○○○○○
COLOR	○○○○○
TASTE	○○○○○

FERTILIZERS & EQUIPMENT

WATER REQUIREMENTS

0%
LESS

CARE INSTRUCTIONS

PLANTING INSTRUCTION

ADDITIONAL NOTES

www.ingramcontent.com/pod-product-compliance
Lightning Source LLC
Chambersburg PA
CBHW050256120526
44590CB00016B/2380